BIRTHDAYS!

CELEBRATING LIFE AROUND THE WORLD

BY EVE B. FELDMAN

CHILDREN'S ART PROVIDED BY PAINTBRUSH DIPLOMACY

BridgeWater Books

Bravo and thanks to all the young artists
who shared their expertise, time, and talent
to make BIRTHDAYS! come alive.

E.B.F.

Mayra Garcia, Age 10 United States of America

Front cover illustration by Mithu Bodan, age 13, India. Back cover illustration by Pya Marchina, age 11, Mexico.

Text copyright © 1996 by Eve B. Feldman.
Illustrations copyright © 1996 by Paintbrush Diplomacy for front and back covers, pages 2,3,5,7,10,13,19,20,22,26,28–29.
Illustrations copyright © 1996 by Troll Communications L.L.C. for pages 4,6,8,9,11,12,14,15,16,17,18,21,23,24,25,27,30–32.

Published by BridgeWater Books, an imprint and trademark of Troll Communications L.L.C.

Library of Congress Cataloging-in-Publication Data
Feldman, Eve, B.
Birthdays!: celebrating life around the world / words by Eve B. Feldman; children's art provided by Paintbrush Diplomacy.
p. cm.
Summary: Simple text and paintings by children show how birthdays are celebrated in different cultures around the world.
ISBN 0–8167–3494–1
1. Birthdays—Pictorial works—Juvenile literature. 2. Children's parties—Pictorial works—Juvenile literature.
[1. Birthdays. 2. Children's art.] I. Paintbrush Diplomacy (Exchange Program). II. Title.
GV1472.7.B5F45 1996 793.2' 1—dc20 95-3631

Dear Reader,

Please come to our celebration which will take you around the world.
You are about to find out how birthdays are observed in different countries.
Everywhere people have found special ways to mark the passing of time
and the miracle of life. In this way, we are all alike. But different countries
have different customs, as you are about to discover. Children from
around the world have created the pictures for this book.
They will show you how THEY celebrate life.

We hope you enjoy our special party!

Karina Schmidt, Age 12 Germany

Birthdays are for spinning around.

Martha Gail Biddiscombe, Age 9   United States of America

Birthdays are for lying on the ground.

Time for sitting in a special chair,

Lucas Bourdrez, Age 11

Happy people making birthday wishes.

Fabio Molinini, Age 11   **Italy**

Happy people eating special dishes.

Bread served with tea, hot enough to steam,

Raseel Sehmi, Age 9   **Ethiopia**

Bread with hot chocolate and curls of whipped cream.

Chocolate balls with sprinkles galore,

Mourrice Papi, Age 8   **Brazil**

Bits of confetti all over the floor.

Lilian Camposano, Age 12

Cake with candles,

Sam Faulkner, Age 10   **England**

Cake with flags,

Or a surprise within.

Kerry Patterson, Age 9 **Scotland**

Blue cornbread,

Marvina Hoskie, Age 10

Seaweed soup,

Hoyeon Kim, Age 6   **Korea**

Or noodles, long and thin.

爷爷长寿 陈迪 十二岁 九四年十月

China

Any color, shape, or spice,

Stephen Zinchack, Age 10   **Nigeria**

Birthday rice is always nice!

Singing and banging with a stick,

Noé Yeshua Santillan, Age 10

Mexico

A choice of presents from which to pick.

Special birthday clothes to wear,

Sakura Stone, Age 11   **Japan**

Time to cut a baby's hair.

Marica Nacuva, Age 13

A time to mark a special age,

Vo Chi Kim Choa, Age 13

Vietnam

Or maybe just a special stage.

Celebrating life and birth–

Roy Nirmalya, Age 13

Everywhere around the earth.

India

Notes

Page 4   United States
In the United States, games such as pin the tail on the donkey are often played at birthday parties. A large poster of a donkey is placed on the wall, and every player gets a turn being blindfolded and spun around and around. The blindfolded person then tries to pin the donkey's tail as close as possible to where it belongs. The one whose donkey's tail comes closest may win a small prize.

Page 5   Egypt
Family and friends traditionally gather when a baby is one week old. Bags of candy, nuts, and raisins are given to the other children present, who may also hold lit candles. The infant is placed on a special screen on the floor. If ancient customs are observed, the mother crosses over the baby, back and forth, while salt is scattered in the air, symbolizing protection for the newborn.

Page 6   Holland
A child in the Netherlands gets to sit on a specially decorated chair for his or her birthday. This chair is covered with *slingers,* which are streamers made of colored paper. In school the boy or girl shares a treat with classmates, and the class sings a birthday song.

Page 7   Israel
In Israel children observe their birthdays by wearing garlands of flowers on their heads. A birthday boy or girl is also lifted up in a chair: the same number of times as his or her new age—plus one for good luck! While this is going on, a birthday song, *"Yom Hooledet,"* is sung, with everyone clapping their hands and stomping their feet in celebration.

Page 8   Italy
"Agure per un Buon Compleanno!" is the Italian phrase for "Good birthday wishes!" In addition to birthday celebrations, many Italians celebrate *onomastico,* or "name day." If a child is named after a saint, he or she may celebrate that saint's day, receiving good wishes and, perhaps, a special treat or sweet. Some saints are remembered with particular foods, such as St. Joseph's cake, a pastry with whipped cream and a cherry on top.

Page 9   Russia
A Russian birthday celebration often includes a meal with family and friends. Chicken with potatoes and mushrooms might be the main dish. If fruit is in season, guests may toast to the health of the birthday person with a drink made from cooked fruit.

Page 10   Ethiopia
In the countryside of Ethiopia, where calendars are not often used, birthdays may not be celebrated at all. But in Ethiopian cities, such as Addis Ababa, piping hot tea is served with a round bread called *dabo.* Slices of *dabo* can be dipped in salt and oil.

Page 11   Denmark
Part of a Danish birthday celebration includes drinking hot chocolate topped with heavy whipped cream. *Boller,* which are round, soft buns filled with raisins and topped with sugar or cinnamon, are also shared.

Lola Campbell, Age 7 United States of America

Page 12   Brazil

Birthday parties in Brazil mean family, friends, and sweets. In addition to cake, there is a special sweet called *brigadeiro,* which is a ball of chocolate mixed with condensed milk and smothered in sprinkles. There are also *cazadinho,* a combination of chocolate and coconut; *quindim,* made from egg yolk, sugar, and coconut; and *olho de sogra,* which is a mixture of coconut and milk with half a plum in the middle.

Page 13   Guatemala

Children in Guatemala eat cake and ice cream for their birthdays. The ice cream is served with a sweet sugar wafer or cone in it. The wafer is called a *barquillo.* The birthday celebration may also include breaking a *piñata:* a papier-mâché figure, often in the shape of an animal, that is filled with treats.

Page 14   England

A birthday cake in England may be decorated according to a theme and topped with candles. The number of candles is the same as the age of the birthday child. It's said that to have his or her wish come true, the birthday boy or girl must blow out all the candles with one breath.

Page 15   Denmark

Flags are another way of announcing a birthday in Denmark. Small red-and-white Danish flags decorate the creamy birthday cake, called *lag kage,* and they may be arranged neatly in the garden as well. There is also a tradition of baking a cake shaped like a boy or a girl. This cake is topped with sugar and candy and has the birthday child's name written on it.

Page 16   Scotland

When making a birthday cake, a parent may wrap a coin in waxed paper or foil and place it in the batter before baking—to be found by a lucky guest when the cake is sliced! In school the birthday child may get a greeting of "nips and dumps." These are pinches and pats, one for each year.

Page 17   Navajo

Rather than celebrate the date of a child's birth, the Navajo traditionally enjoy celebrations of landmarks in a boy's or girl's life. Blue bread, melon, squash, and mutton are some of the foods that may be shared during such a celebration. Blue bread, made of corn mixed with ashes from burnt sage or cedar, is sometimes baked in an outdoor oven.

Page 18   Korea

Seaweed soup is one of the first foods served to a new mother in Korea. Seaweed contains a lot of iron, which is an important source of strength. The soup frequently is included at birthday celebrations, too.

Page 19   China

Birthdays in China are traditionally celebrated for adults who have reached at least sixty years of age. Instead of a cake, *lo mein* noodles are eaten. The noodles' length suggests a long life.

Page 20   Nigeria

Nigeria is one of many countries where rice is part of a birthday celebration. There may be rice with beef and prawns, rice with chicken, or rice with fresh fish. In the western part of Nigeria, the person whose birthday is being celebrated often wears an elegant version of the traditional outfit: *shkto buba* for a boy or man; *buba* for a girl or woman.

Page 21   Haiti

Birthday parties are usually held outdoors in this Caribbean nation. Rice and beans, or rice with meat or chicken, are served. The birthday cake does not have candles, but it is often covered with brightly colored icing.

Page 22   Mexico

A *piñata* is an important part of Mexican birthday celebrations. *Piñatas* can be made at home or bought in a store. Before the party the *piñata* is stuffed full of candy and small toys. Children take turns hitting the *piñata* so candy and toys spill out for everyone to share. The traditional song *"Las Mañanitas"* is sung.

Page 23   Korea

A baby in Korea is already considered a one-year-old at birth. One year after the baby's birth, his or her family holds an elaborate party. The baby wears special clothes and receives all kinds of presents. Everyone watches which present the baby will try to reach for. If it's a book, perhaps the baby will grow up to be a teacher or a scholar. If it's a gold coin, maybe the baby will become a banker. Guests have fun making these predictions as they enjoy rice cake and seaweed soup.

Page 24   Japan

Every November 15, the holiday of *Shichi-go-san* is celebrated for three-year-old boys and girls, five-year-old boys, and seven-year-old girls. Children of these ages wear traditional kimonos and go with their families to a local shrine to pray for their health and happiness. They are then given special "1000-year-candy"—with the hope that eating it will bring them a thousand years of health and happiness.

Page 25   Fiji

At about the time of a baby's first birthday on the island of Fiji, a special celebration takes place when the child receives his or her first haircut. The baby wears the traditional *tapa* dress, and the honor of cutting the hair goes to an esteemed relative.

Page 26   Vietnam

Traditionally the most important birthdays in Vietnam are those at the first month and the first year of life. Prayers and incense are part of these celebrations, and ancestors are remembered in the prayers. After the age of sixty, adults celebrate birthdays by decades.

Page 27   Navajo

Navajo celebrations center around landmarks such as a baby's first smile or a first laugh. Another landmark celebration is *kinaalda,* which marks the time when a girl becomes a woman. Each day for about a week, the girl runs toward the sun, running farther and farther every day. The medicine man sings special songs for her, and a corn cake is shared.

Page 28   India

In the countryside of India, birthdays are usually celebrated with a visit to the temple. In cities like Bombay, Delhi, and Calcutta, there may be large birthday parties with birthday cakes, birthday balloons, and horns.